The Trapp Family
Book of Christmas Songs

Selected and arranged by Franz Wasner and illustrated by Agathe Trapp

Pantheon Books · New York

ACKNOWLEDGMENTS

The Publishers herewith thank:

The Librairie Beauchemin, Montreal, Canada, for permission to reprint the text and melody of "Whence, O Shepherd Maiden," from *Canadian Folk Songs*.

Richard Chase, Big Stove Gap, Virginia, for permission to print the music of "As Joseph Was A-Walking" and "The Seven Joys of Mary" from manuscript.

The Church Pension Fund, New York City, for permission to reprint the English text of "He, Whom Joyous Shepherds Praised" from hymns Nos. 35 and 322 in *The Hymnal*, 1940.

Henry S. Drinker, Philadelphia, Penna., for permission to print his translation of "Maria Walks Amid the Thorn" from manuscript.

The E. M. Lohmann Co., Saint Paul, Minnesota, for permission to reprint the English text of "Jesus, Redeemer of the World" from *The Saint Andrew Daily Missal*.

Novello & Co., Ltd., London, England, for permission to reprint the melody of "The Holly and the Ivy," collected and arranged by Cecil J. Sharp, copyright 1913 by Novello & Co., Ltd.

The Oxford University Press, London, England, for permission to reprint the English text of the "Rocking Song" from *The Oxford Book of Carols*.

John Powell, Richmond, Virginia, for permission to print the text of "The Seven Joys of Mary" from manuscript.

G. Schirmer, Inc., New York City, for permission to reprint the English text of "Bring Your Torches, Jeannette, Isabella" from *Christmas Carols from Many Countries,* arranged by Satis N. Coleman and Elin K. Jorgensen, copyright 1934 by G. Schirmer Inc., and the English text of the "Carol of the Bagpipers" from *Songs of Italy*, English translation by Dr. Theodore Baker, copyright 1904 by G. Schirmer, Inc.

The editor expresses his special thanks to Miss Hester Root for most valuable help in translating many of the foreign songs into English.

Table of Contents

The "Gloria in Excelsis" Throughout the Ages

IN HOLY SCRIPTURES, we read of a world of spirits, the nine choirs of angels. Frequently they are sent by God into the lives of men. We see them visiting Abraham, accompanying Tobias, wrestling with Jacob, announcing the birth of the Saviour and of John the Baptist, His forerunner, bringing counsel repeatedly to Joseph in his sleep, serving the Saviour in the desert, strengthening Him at the beginning of His suffering in the garden, announcing His glorious resurrection and prophesying His second coming after His ascension.

But in all these meetings between angels and men, only once, one single time, have men heard the angels *sing:* in Bethlehem in that holy, silent night after the herald angel had announced: "Fear nothing, for behold I bring you good tidings of great joy . . . for this day is born to you a Saviour . . ." There was with Him suddenly a multitude of the heavenly host. This heavenly choir sang the first Christmas carol of all times: *Gloria in excelsis Deo, et in terra pax hominibus bonae voluntatis.* And these lucky shepherds were the only mortals who have heard angels sing.

For two thousand years man has tried feebly to reproduce the sound of the first Gloria. To some, the heavenly army seemingly sang in unison, one mighty, long-drawn sound like a call from heaven to earth; others felt it rather as a polyphonic pattern, ups and downs of innumerable jubilant voices; others again seemed to hear clear homophonic chords; and again others felt sure there must have been a great antiphonal between that "angel of the Lord" and the multitude—the soloist and the choir.

The Christmas carols of all times and peoples keep strictly to the narrative of St. Luke, which has three distinct points: The recitative of the Angel of the Lord—The choir of the multitudes of angels—The reaction of the shepherds.

There are Christmas hymns dealing only with the "good tidings of great joy," the birth of Christ the Lord with the descriptions of the Infant wrapped in swaddling clothes and laid in a manger, the young mother kneeling beside Him singing Him to sleep with a lullaby.

There are the carols in all tongues of this world promising peace to men and praising God in a never-ending Gloria.

And there are finally those lovely songs describing the reaction of the human heart to the heavenly message—the shepherds' songs of many lands, commemorating what those uncomplicated, unsophisticated hearts said to one another: "Let us go over to Bethlehem," and how they came "with haste" and found Mary and Joseph and the Infant in the manger; and the centuries and nations go to work upon what must have gone on in the hearts of those shepherds; and although the shepherds from the Tyrolean highlands may express it a little differently from their brothers in Italy or in the plains of Hungary, fundamentally it is the same: wonder, love, adoration, and the wish to help, to serve. So these carols describe the shepherds running over to the cave bringing their gifts: bread, milk, and butter, a sheepskin as a coverlet for the shivering Baby.

Singing at Christmas goes back to the early centuries of Christianity. It is the oldest of those innumerable folk customs still alive throughout the world during the Christmas season. Books have been filled, years have been spent in research on this subject. We shall only mention here what we have heard and seen ourselves on our extensive travels through many lands of different continents. First of all, we have made one great discovery: while other folk customs, for instance those around weddings or burials, have strictly national features, we have found the same lovely folklore around Christmas in many countries.

Among the more wide-spread institutions are:

THE ADVENT WREATH, a big wreath of fir twigs (laurel or holly in the hot countries), on which are fastened four candles. The Christmas season begins four weeks before Christmas Eve, on the Feast of the First Sunday in Advent, and each of the four candles is for one Advent Sunday. This wreath hangs from the ceiling of the living room, and the family gathers under it in the evenings and sings carols.

THE ADVENT CANDLE, a tall, thick candle, the symbol of Christ, the Light of the World, is lit in the homes in these weeks of preparation.

THE CRÈCHE, which has become universally loved and used in homes and churches throughout the Christian world. As will be seen later, we have St. Francis of Assisi to thank for it. His great desire to celebrate the Christmas feast with special warmth and devotion took root and perpetuated itself everywhere. In cathedrals and abbeys solemn Matins are chanted, and Midnight service has become the heart of the feast for every adult Christian.

Almost as old as the singing of carols is the habit of giving gifts at Christmas time, in commemoration of the gifts the shepherds brought to the Christ-child. In England and America, gifts are distributed and the tree is lighted on the morning of December 25th. In Germany, Austria, Poland and the Scandinavian countries this is done on Christmas Eve.

THE CHRISTMAS TREE seems like the prophecy of Isaias come true: "The glory of Lebanon shall come unto thee, the fir tree, the pine tree, . . . to beautify the place of my sanctuary" (Isaias 60,13). It, too, is a symbol of Christ as the Tree of Life.

CANDLES all over the house at Christmas are also found in the early centuries. Saint Jerome mentions them as an expression of Christmas joy.

THE HOLLY AND THE IVY, THE MISTLETOE AND THE YULE LOG are symbols which have their roots in pagan times and have become a part of the Christmas celebration in many lands now; also the baking of special cakes and cookies and the sending of greeting cards.

The vivid descriptions in some of the carols lead by themselves to dramatizations of the events, and so we find very early Christmas plays, especially shepherd plays. They began as Mystery plays in church, performed in the sanctuary before Midnight Mass. Soon they found their way into the homes of the faithful.

A lovely custom is enacted in many countries, the search for shelter of Mary and Joseph in Bethlehem. We found it mostly in the Alps—the *Herbergsuchen,* and in Mexico—the *Posada.* Nine days before Christmas it begins. Many families gather together, a procession is formed. The statues of Mary and Joseph are carried, everybody bearing a lighted candle because it is after dark. Every night the procession stops before another home, and Mary and Joseph ask pleadingly for admission. The host answers from inside very harshly, and during verse after verse he refuses to let them in, until he finally discovers who they are, and most embarrassedly apologizes and opens his house wide for the illustrious guests. The statues are carried to a place of honor, where they are kept twenty-four hours in a mass of candles. The whole crowd kneels and prays and sings. Afterwards there is a party and great rejoicing.

After Christmas Day itself, the second highest feastday of the season is Epiphany, the Feast of the Three Holy Kings. In many countries gifts are given on that day, in imitation of the Three Wise Men in Bethlehem. Another folk dramatization is enacted on that day, the "Star-singing." After dark, little groups of three men dressed as the Three Holy Kings—one white, one brown, one black—one of them carrying a big star on a stick, go from house to house caroling, and receive gifts of Christmas cake and dried fruit in exchange.

On Epiphany also there is the Blessing of the Homes. The whole family, led by the father, who carries a pan with incense, goes through all the rooms of the house, through all the barns and stables, and over every entrance the father of the house writes with blessed chalk the letters: C. M. B., the initials of the Three Holy Kings, Caspar, Melchior, and Balthazar, thus keeping evil influences away from his home.

Some countries have their special customs:

In France, Christmas is predominantly a religious feast; the gift-giving day is Epiphany. Crèches are put up in homes and churches. Midnight Mass is attended by large crowds and celebrated with great solemnity. Groups sing in the streets during the Christmas season, and money is tossed to them from windows. There is a large number of French Christmas carols, which are called "Noels," the term being derived from *natalis i.e. dies*, the birthday of Christ. In some parts of France, young people still dress as shepherds and shepherdesses and come with drums and pipes to the church for Midnight Mass, carrying torches to find the way (see the carol on p. 94, "Bring Your Torches, Jeannette, Isabella").

The Italian Christmas received its most powerful inspiration from St. Francis of Assisi on Christmas Eve 1223, near Greccio in Umbria, an inspiration which did not remain confined within the borders of Italy, but spread over the whole Christian world. It was three years before his death, and Francis desired, as his biographer Bonaventura tells us, "to re-enact the birth of Christ in order to move the people to devotion." Close to the Castle of Greccio was a cave which the Saint turned into a stable like that in which Jesus was born. A manger was built and filled with hay, and on Christmas Eve an ox and ass were led into the cave to stand on either side of the manger, and with the Pope's permission Mass was celebrated at midnight over the manger. Francis himself served as deacon and preached to the people, standing in front of the manger, "full with the sweet love of God and the greatest devotion." He had invited many of the brothers and also the people from the neighboring towns and hills and they came in great numbers, so "that the entire forest was bright with the light of many torches and resounded with the singing of solemn songs of praise."

The custom of the "crib" or "crèche" ("Krippe" in German, "nacimiento" in Spanish) has spread rapidly into other countries and is still very much alive in Italy, Austria, Bavaria, France, Spain, and Mexico.

In accordance with the Latin tradition, the time for gaiety and gifts and the enjoyment of children in Italy is the Feast of the Epiphany, January 6, Twelfth Night, and its octave, with street celebrations, noisy instruments, and many stories about the fairy "La Befana" (derived from Epiphany), from whom the children expect gifts.

In Sweden, one of the special features of Christmas is the dance around the Christmas tree. Children and adults join hands and sing the Dance Carol (see page 112).

In Poland, Christmas carols are called "Kolendy" (singular Kolenda). They are sung in the homes when, on Christmas Eve, everybody joins hands after dinner and walks around the tree; in the churches at Midnight Mass; and all through the Christmas season which lasts until Epiphany or Candlemas. Under the tree is the "crib," and the tree is decorated with many decorations homemade during the Advent season. There are many quaint customs and observances connected with Christmas dinner, as, for instance, putting hay under the table cloth, breaking the waifer, etc.

While I am writing this, I listen to the sound of the bells in the nearby St. Theresita's Church playing—of all things—"Hark the Herald Angels Sing." We are in Caracas, Venezuela, on a concert tour through South America, and the words of Phillips Brooks come to my mind:

Christmas in lands of the fir tree and pine;
Christmas in lands of the palm tree and vine;
Christmas where snow peaks stand solemn and white;
Christmas where corn fields lie sunny and bright;
Everywhere, everywhere, Christmas tonight.

MARIA AUGUSTA TRAPP

Jerusalem Rejoice / Jerusalem Gaude

Gregorian antiphon

ca. 600

Moderato maestoso

Je—ru—sa—lem re — joice, be glad and joy — ful,
Je—ru—sa—lem gau — de gau-di—o ma — gno,

for there shall come un—to thee a Sav — iour, al—le — lu — ja.
qui — a ve — ni—et ti—bi Sal—va—tor, al—le — lu — ja.

Jesus, Redeemer of the World / Jesu Redemptor Omnium

Ambrosian chant

Sixth century

Maestoso

Je — sus, Re — deem — er of the world,
Je — su, Re — dem — ptor om — ni — um,

Who, ere the ear—liest dawn of light, Wast from e — ter–nal ag–es born,
Quem lu—cis an—te o—ri — gi — nem, Pa — rem pa — ter–nae glo—ri — ae,

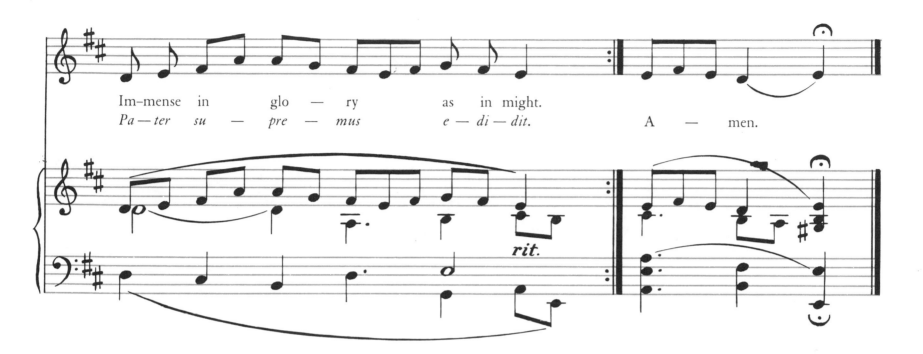

Im—mense in glo — ry as in might.
Pa — ter su — pre — mus e — di — dit.
A — men.

This ever blest recurring day
Its witness bears, that all alone,
From Thy own Father's bosom forth,
To save the world Thou camest down.

O Day! to which the seas and sky,
And earth, and heav'n, glad welcome sing;
O Day! which heal'd our misery,
And brought on earth salvation's King.

O Jesus, born of virgin bright,
Immortal glory be to Thee;
Praise to the Father infinite
And Holy Ghost eternally.

Testatur hoc praesens dies,
Currens per anni circulum,
Quod solus e sinu Patris
Mundi salus adveneris.

Hunc astra, tellus, aequora,
Hunc omne quod caelo subest,
Salutis auctorem novae
Novo salutat cantico.

Jesu, tibi sit gloria,
Qui natus es de virgine,
Cum Padre et almo Spiritu,
In sempiterna saecula.

A Child is Born in Bethlehem / Puer Natus in Bethlehem

Latin carol

Fourteenth century

Allegro moderato

A Child is born in Beth — le — hem, Beth — le — hem, And
Pu — er na — tus in Beth — le — hem, Beth — le — hem, Un —

joy is in Je — ru — sa — lem. Al — le — lu — ja, al — le — lu — ja.
de gau — det Je — ru — sa — lem.

Per Gabrielem nuntium
Virgo concepit Filium.

Assumpsit carnem Filius
Dei Patris Altissimus.

Reges de Saba veniunt,
Aurum, thus, myrrham offerunt.

Laudetur sancta Trinitas,
Deo dicamus gratias.

Through Gabriel sent from Heav'n above,
A virgin bore a Son with love.

In flesh appeared the Holy Son
Of God the Father, Mighty One.

Three Holy Kings of Orient
Gold, frankincense, and myrrh present.

Praise to the Holy Trinity,
Thanksgiving unto God most high.

He, Whom Joyous Shepherds Praised / Quem Pastores Laudavere

Ad quem magi ambulabant,
Aurum, thus, myrrham portabant,
Immolabant haec sincere
Nato Regi Gloriae.

Exsultemus cum Maria,
In caelesti hierarchia
Natum promat voce pia
Dulci cum melodia.

Christo regi, Deo nato,
Per Mariam nobis dato,
Merito resonet vere
Laus, honor et gloria.

He, whom sages, westward faring,
Myrrh and gold and incense bearing,
Worshiped, bowing low before him,
Reigns as King this happy morn.

Now rejoice with Jesus' mother,
Praise her newborn son, and brother,
Angels vie with one another,
Praising Him beyond the sky.

Sing to Christ, the King who reigneth,
Yet of Mary manhood gaineth,
Born our God; let us adore Him:
Glory be to God on high.

Carol of the Nuns of Saint Mary's, Chester

English macaronic carol

Teneramente

He who heav'n cre — at — ed,

Jo — seph he bought the swad—dling clothes,

Qui cre — a — vit cae — lum,

Jo — seph e — mit pan — ni — cu — lum,

Lul — ly, lul — ly, lu,

Born is He in sta — ble stall,

Ma — ry the moth — er kind and mild,

Na — sci — tur in sta — bu — lo,

Ma — ter in — vol — vit Pu — e — rum,

Bye, bye, bye, bye, bye,

He the King Who rul — eth all,
In — to the crib she put the Child,
Rex qui re — git sae — cu — lum,
Et po — nit in prae — se — pi — o,
Lul — ly, lul — ly lu.

Jesus at His mother's breast,
She doth kiss her Child and Lord,
And adores th' Incarnate Word.

Mother, pray thy Holy Son,
That He give us of His joy,
That we heav'nly life enjoy.

Lactat Mater Dominum,
Osculatur parvulum,
Et adorat Dominum.

Roga mater Filium
Ut det nobis gaudium,
In perenni gloria.

17

O Come, All Ye Faithful / Adeste Fideles

Latin carol

Traditional

Maestoso

O come, all ye faith—ful, joy—ful and tri—um—phant, O
Ad — es — te fi—de—les, lae—ti tri—um—phan—tes, Ve —

come ye, o come ye to Beth — le—hem! Come and be—hold Him,
ni — te, ve — ni—te in Beth — le—hem! Na — tum vi—de — te

born the King of An — gels: O come let us a — dore Him, o come let us a—
Re—gem an-ge — lo — rum: Ve ni — te ad—o — re—mus, ve — ni — te ad — o—

dore Him, O come let us a — dore Him, Christ the Lord!
re — mus, Ve — ni — te ad — o — re — mus Do — mi—num.

See how the shepherds, summon'd to His cradle,
Leaving their flocks, drew nigh with holy fear.
We too shall thither bend our joyful footsteps: *Refrain*

Sing, choirs of angels, sing in exultation,
Sing, all ye citizens of heav'n above:
Glory to God, glory in the highest: *Refrain*

Yea, Lord, we greet Thee, born this happy morning,
Jesus, to Thee be glory giv'n:
Word of the Father, now in flesh appearing: *Refrain*

En grege relicto, humiles ad cunas
Vocati pastores approperant.
Et nos ovanti gradu festinemus: Refrain

Cantet nunc Io! chorus angelorum;
Cantet nunc aula caelestium:
Gloria, gloria, in excelsis Deo: Refrain

Ergo qui natus die hodierna,
Jesu, tibi sit gloria!
Patris aeterni Verbum caro factum: Refrain

O Publish the Glad Story / Célébrons la Naissance

French macaronic carol

Seventeenth-century air

Con spirito

O pub — lish the glad sto—ry   No — stri   Sal—va—to — ris,   Who
Cé — lé — brons la nais—san—ce

is   the joy and glo—ry   De — i   su—i Pa — tris   This In — fant pure and ho—ly   In
fait   la com—plai—san—ce   Cet En — fant tout ai—ma—ble

noc — te me—di — a
Is born in sta—ble low—ly
Est ne dans une é—ta—ble
De ca — sta Ma—ri — a.

Those happy tidings ringing
Olim pastoribus
By angels sweetly singing
Fuit nuntiatus
O leave your sheep to pasture
In agro viridi,
O come adore your Master
Filiumque Dei.

Th' angelic choir rejoices
Juncti pastoribus,
They sing with heav'nly voices:
Puer vobis natus
To God who did conceive men
Gloria in excelsis
And peace on earth doth give them
Bonae voluntatis.

Cette heureuse nouvelle
Olim pastoribus
Par un ange fidèle
Fuit nuntiatus,
Leur disant laissez paître
In agro viridi
Venez voir votre maître
Filiumque Dei.

Mille esprits angéliques
Juncti pastoribus,
Chantent dans leur musique:
Puer vobis natus,
Au dieu par qui nous sommes
Gloria in excelsis,
Et la paix soit aux hommes
Bonae voluntatis.

Sing, O Sing! / Psallite Unigenito

Latin carol of German origin (see note)

Allegretto

Sing,   o   sing!   Hail the Ho—ly One!   Je—sus Christ, of God the Son,
Psal — li — te   *U — ni-ge—ni — to,*   *Chri-sto De—i Fi—li - o,*

Sing,   o   sing!   For our sins He doth a—tone, This   in—fant Son, In man—ger   crib He's all   a—lone.
Psal—li — te   *Re-demp-to — ri Do—mi—no,   Pu — e—ru—lo,   Ja—cen—ti   in prae—se—pi—o.*

Fine

A ti—ny In—fant dear Lies in a man—ger drear. An—gels bright from heav'n—ly sphere In
Ein klei—nes Kin—de—lein Liegt in dem Krip—pe—lein. Al — le lie—ben En — ge—lein Die—

lov—ing watch ap—pear, An—gels bright from heav'n—ly sphere Sing prais — es far and near.
nen dem Kin—de—lein, Al — le lie—ben En — ge—lein Sin — gen dem Kind—lein fein.

%. to Fine

%. to Fine

The First Noel

English carol

Seventeenth century

The first No — el, the an—gel did say,
Was to cer—tain poor

They look — ed up and saw a star
Shin–ing in the

shep–herds in fields as they lay; In fields where they lay keep—ing their

East, be — yond them far, And to where the earth it gave their great

sheep, On a cold win—ter's night that was so deep.
No — el, No—
light, And so it con — tin—ued both day and night.

el, No — el, No — el! Born is the King of Is — ra — el!

26

And by the light of that same star,
Three wise men came from country far;
To seek for a king was their intent,
And to follow the star wherever it went. *Refrain*

This star drew nigh to the northwest,
Over Bethlehem it took its rest,
And there it did both stop and stay,
Right over the place where Jesus lay. *Refrain*

Then entered in those wise men three,
Full reverently upon the knee,
And offered there, in His presence,
Their gold, and myrrh, and frankincense. *Refrain*

Then let us all, with one accord,
Sing praises to our heavenly Lord,
Who hath made heaven and earth of nought,
And with His blood mankind hath bought. *Refrain*

God Rest You Merry, Gentlemen

English carol

Eighteenth-century air

we were gone a — stray.
noth—ing take in scorn.   O   tid — ings of com — fort and joy, com–fort and
Son of God by name.

joy, O tid — ings of com — fort and joy.

And when they came to Bethlehem
Where our dear Saviour lay,
They found Him in a manger,
Where oxen feed on hay;
His Mother Mary kneeling down,
Unto the Lord did pray. *Refrain*

Now to the Lord sing praises,
All you within this place,
And with true love and brotherhood
Each other now embrace;
This holy tide of Christmas
All other doth deface. *Refrain*

Deck the Hall

English carol

Old Welsh air

Allegretto

Deck the hall with boughs of hol—ly,
See the blaz—ing Yule be—fore us, Fa la la la la la
Fast a—way the old year pass—es,

la la la. 'Tis the sea—son to be jol—ly,
Strike the lamp and join the cho—rus, Fa la la la la la la la la.
Hail the new, ye lads and lass—es,

Don we now our gay ap–par — el,
Fol — low me in mer — ry meas—ure,   Fa la la   la la la   la la la.
Sing we joy — ous all to–geth — er,

Troll the an — cient Yule — tide car — ol,
While I tell of Yule — tide treas—ure,   Fa la la la la   la la la.
Heed — less of the wind and weath—er,

Coventry Carol

English carol

Seventeenth century or earlier

Lento

Lul — ly, lul — la, thou lit—tle ti — ny child,

By by, lul — ly lul — lay. Thou lit — tle ti—ny child, By by, lul — ly lul—lay.

O sis—ters too, How may we do For to pre — serve this day This
He — rod the king, In his rag — ing, Charg-ed he hath this day His
That woe is me, Poor child for thee! And ev-er morn and day, For

poor young — ling For whom we do sing? By by, lul — ly lul — lay.
men of might, In his own sight, All young chil — dren to slay.
thy part — ing Nei—ther say nor sing By by, lul — ly lul — lay

The Holly and the Ivy

English carol

Traditional

The hol—ly and the i—vy, When they are both full grown, Of all the trees that are
The hol—ly bears a blos—som, As white as the lil—y flow'r, And Ma—ry bore sweet
The hol—ly bears a ber—ry, As red as a—ny blood, And Ma—ry bore sweet

in the wood, The hol—ly bears the crown:
Je—sus Christ, To be our sweet Sav—iour: The ris—ing of the sun And the
Je—sus Christ, To do poor sin—ners good:

run-ning of the deer, The play-ing of the mer-ry or—gan, Sweet sing-ing in the choir.

The holly bears a prickle,
As sharp as any thorn,
And Mary bore sweet Jesus Christ
On Christmas day in the morn: *Refrain*

The holly bears a bark,
As bitter as any gall,
And Mary bore sweet Jesus Christ
For to redeem us all: *Refrain*

Wassail Song

English carol

Poem by J. M. Neale (1818-1866); sixteenth-century air

Here we come a — was—sail—ing A — mong the leaves so green,
We are not dai — ly beg — gars That beg from door to door, But
God bless the mas — ter of this house, Like — wise the mis — tress too, And
Good Mas — ter and good Mis — tress, While you're sit — ting by the fire,

Here we come a — wan—der—ing, So fair to be seen:
we are neigh—bors' chil — dren Whom you have seen be — fore:
all the lit — tle chil — dren That round the ta — ble go:
Pray think of us poor chil—dren Who are wand—'ring in the mire:

Love and joy come to

you, And to you your was — sail too, And God bless you and send you A

hap — py New Year, And God send you a hap — py New Year.

Good King Wenceslas

English carol

Poem by William Dix (1837-1898); Sixteenth-century air

Allegro moderato

Good King Wen–ces – las look'd out On the Feast of Steph — en,
'Hith — er, page, and stand by me, If thou know'st it, tell — ing,
'Bring me flesh and bring me wine, Bring me pine logs hith — er;

When the snow lay round a—bout, Deep and crisp and e — ven; Bright — ly shone the
Yon — der peas—ant who is he? Where and what his dwell–ing?' 'Sire, he lives a
Thou and I shall see him dine When we bear them thith—er.' Page and mon — arch

moon that night, Though the frost was cru — el, When a poor man came in sight,
good league hence, Un — der—neath the moun — tain; Right a — gainst the for — est fence,
forth they went, Forth they went to — geth—er; Through the rude wind's wild la—ment

Gath—'ring win — ter fu — el.
By Saint Ag—nes' foun — tain.'
And the bit—ter weath — er.

'Sire, the night is darker now,
And the wind blows stronger;
Fails my heart, I know not how,
I can go no longer.'
'Mark my footsteps, my good page,
Tread thou in them boldly:
Thou shalt find the winter's rage
Freeze thy blood less coldly.'

In his master's steps he trod,
Where the snow lay dinted;
Heat was in the very sod
Which the saint had printed;
Therefore, Christian men, be sure,
Wealth or rank possessing,
Ye who now will bless the poor,
Shall yourselves find blessing.

What Child Is This?

English

Fifteenth century

Moderato

What Child is this, who, laid to rest On Ma — ry's lap, is
Why lies He in such mean es-tate, Where ox and ass are
So bring Him in — cense, gold, and myrrh, Come peas — ant, King to

sleep — ing? Whom an — gels greet with an — thems sweet, While shep — herds watch are
feed — ing? Good Chris — tians fear: for sin — ners here The si — lent Word is
own Him; The King of Kings sal — va — tion brings; Let lov — ing hearts en—

keep—ing?
plead—ing.
throne Him!

This, this is Christ the King, Whom shep—herds guard and an—gels sing:

Haste, haste to bring Him laud, The Babe, the Son of Ma — ry.

Hark! the Herald Angels Sing

English carol

Maestoso

Poem by Charles Wesley (1707-1788); music by Felix Mendelssohn (1809-1847)

Hark! the her — ald an—gels sing, "Glo—ry to the new–born King!
Christ, by high — est heav'n a–dor'd, Christ, the ev — er—last—ing Lord;
Mild, He lays His glo—ry by, Born that man no more may die;

Peace on earth, and mer—cy mild; God and sin — ners rec — on–cil'd!" Joy—ful, all ye
Long de—sir'd, be—hold Him come, Find—ing here His hum—ble home. Veil'd in flesh the
Born to raise the sons of earth, Born to give them sec—ond birth. Ris'n with heal—ing

As Joseph Was A-Walking

American folk carol

Traditional English poem

As Jos—eph was a—walk—ing, he heard an an — gel sing: This
He nei—ther shall be born — ed in house nor in the hall, Nor
He nei—ther shall be wash—en in white wine nor in red, But

night shall be the birth—night of Christ, the heav'n–ly King; This
in a King's pal — ace, but in an ox—en's stall; Nor
in the clear spring wa — ter with which we were chris–ten — ed. But

44

night   shall be the birth — night of Christ, the heav'n–ly King.
in   a King's   pal — ace, but in an ox—en's stall.
in   the clear spring wa — ter with which we were chris–ten — ed.

He neither shall be clothed in purple nor in pall,
But in the fair white linen that usen babies all.

He neither shall be rocked in silver nor in gold,
But in a wooden cradle that rocks upon the mold.

On the sixth day of January His birthday shall be,
When the stars and the elements shall tremble with glee.

As Joseph was a-walking, thus did the angel sing;
And Mary's Son at midnight was born to be our King.

The Seven Joys of Mary

American folk carol   *Quasi recitativo*

Fifteenth-century English poem

The first joy of Ma—ry was the joy of one: That the bless—ed
The next joy of Ma—ry was the joy of two: That her Son
The next joy of Ma—ry was the joy of three: That her Son

Je — sus was born to be her Son, Born to be her Son, O my
Je — sus could read the Scrip — ture through, Read the Scrip — ture through, O my
Je — sus could make the blind to see, Make the blind to see, O my

Fa — ther in glo — ry, Born to be her Son.
Fa — ther in glo — ry, Read the Scrip—ture through.
Fa — ther in glo — ry, Make the blind to see.

The next joy of Mary was the joy of four:
That her Son Jesus could turn the rich to poor. *Refrain*

The next joy of Mary was the joy of five:
That her Son Jesus could raise the dead alive. *Refrain*

The next joy of Mary was the joy of six:
That her Son Jesus could bear the crucifix. *Refrain*

The last joy of Mary was the joy of seven:
That her Son Jesus could open the gates of heaven. *Refrain*

It Came upon the Midnight Clear

American carol

Allegretto moderato

Poem by Edmund H. Sears (1810-1876); music by Richard S. Willis (1819-1900)

It came up—on the mid—night clear, That glo—rious song of old, From an—gels bend—ing
Still thro' the clo—ven skies they come, With peace—ful wings un—furl'd, And still their heav'n—ly
And ye, be—neath life's crush—ing load, Whose forms are bend—ing low, Who toil a—long the

near the earth To touch their harps of gold: 'Peace on the earth, good—will to men From
mu—sic floats O'er all the wea—ry world: A—bove its sad and low—ly plains They
climb—ing way With pain—ful steps and slow, Look now! for glad and gold—en hours Come

heav'n's all gra — cious King'; The world in sol — emn still—ness lay To hear the an — gels sing.
bend on hov — 'ring wing, And ev — er o'er its Ba—bel sounds The bless–ed an — gels sing.
swift — ly on the wing: O rest be–side the wea – ry road, And hear the an — gels sing.

For lo, the days are hast'ning on,
By prophet bards foretold,
When with the ever-circling years
Comes round the age of gold;

When peace shall over all the earth
Its ancient splendor fling,
And the whole world give back the song
Which now the angels sing.

O Little Town of Bethlehem

American carol

Poem by Phillips Brooks (1828-1893); music by Louis H. Redner (1831-1908)

Andante

O lit—tle town of Beth—le—hem, How still we see thee lie! A—bove thy deep and
For Christ is born of Ma—ry; And gath—er'd all a—bove, While mor—tals sleep, the
O ho—ly Child of Beth—le—hem, De—scend to us we pray; Cast out our sin and

dream—less sleep The si—lent stars go by; Yet in thy dark streets shin—eth The
an—gels keep Their watch of wond—'ring love. O morn—ing stars! to—geth—er Pro—
en—ter in, Be born in us to—day! We hear the Christ—mas an—gels The

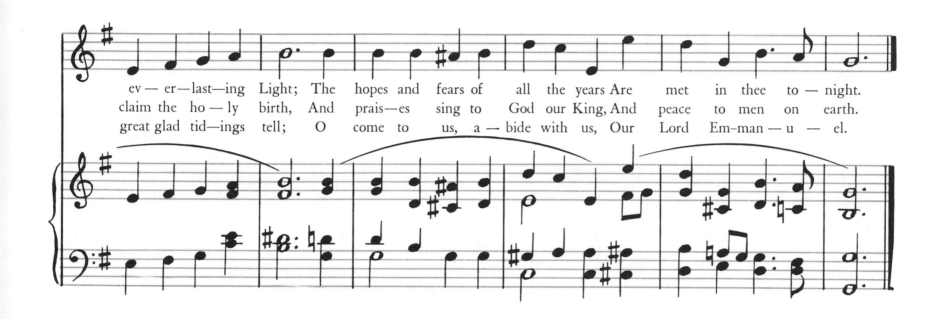

ev — er—last—ing Light; The hopes and fears of all the years Are met in thee to — night.
claim the ho — ly birth, And prais—es sing to God our King, And peace to men on earth.
great glad tid—ings tell; O come to us, a — bide with us, Our Lord Em-man — u — el.

We Three Kings of Orient Are

American carol

Poem and music by John H. Hopkins Jr. (1820-1891)

Star of Night, Star with roy—al beau—ty bright, West-ward lead-ing, Still pro-ceed-ing, Guide us to thy

per—fect light.

'Myrrh is mine; its bitter perfume
Breathes a life of gathering gloom;
Sorrowing, sighing, bleeding, dying,
Seal'd in the stone-cold tomb.' *Refrain*

Glorious now behold Him arise,
King, and God, and Sacrifice;
Heav'n sings Allelujah: Alle-
Lujah the earth replies. *Refrain*

53

Away in a Manger

American carol

Moderato

Nineteenth century

A — way in a man — ger, no crib for a bed, The lit — tle Lord
The cat — tle are low — ing, the poor Ba — by wakes, But lit — tle Lord
Be near me, Lord Je — sus, I ask Thee to stay Close by me for—

Je — sus lay down His sweet head. The stars in the sky look'd
Je — sus no cry — ing He makes. I love Thee, Lord Je — sus, look
ev — er and love me, I pray! Bless all the dear chil — dren in

down where He lay, The lit — tle Lord Je — sus, a — sleep in the hay.
down from the sky, And stay by my cra — dle, till morn — ing is nigh!
Thy ten — der care, And take us to heav — en, to live with Thee there.

Joy to the World

American carol

English poem (by Isaac Watts, 1674-1748); setting by Lowell Mason (1792-1872)

Joy to the world! the Lord is come. Let earth re — ceive her
Joy to the world! the Sav—iour reigns. Let men their songs em —
He rules the world with truth and grace, And makes the na — tions

King. Let ev — 'ry heart pre—pare Him room, And heav'n and na—ture
ploy. While fields and floods, rocks, hills, and plains Re — peat the sound-ing
prove The glo—ries of His right-eous-ness, and won-ders of His love, And won—ders of His

sing, And heav'n and na—ture sing, And heav'n, and heav'n and na—ture sing.
joy, Re — peat the sound-ing joy, Re — peat, re — peat the sound-ing joy.
love, And won—ders of His love, And won — ders, won — ders of His love.

Behold a Branch Is Growing / Es ist ein Ros entsprungen

German carol

Fifteenth century or earlier; harmonization by Praetorius (1571-1621)

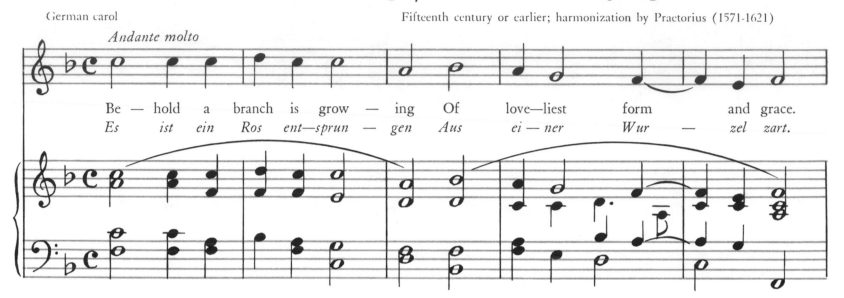

Be — hold a branch is grow — ing Of love—liest form and grace.
Es ist ein Ros ent—sprun — gen Aus ei — ner Wur — zel zart.

As proph—ets sung, fore—know — ing, It springs from Jes — se's race. And bears one
Wie uns die Al—ten sun — gen, Aus Jes — se kam die Art. Und hat ein

lit — tle flow'r   In midst of   cold—est   win — ter, At   deep—est   mid — night hour.

Blüm—lein bracht,   *Mit—ten im   kal—ten   Win — ter, Wohl   zu der   hal — ben Nacht.*

Isaiah hath foretold it
In words of promise sure,
And Mary's arms enfold it,
A Virgin meek and pure.
Through God's eternal will,
This Child to her is given
At midnight calm and still.

Das Röslein, das ich meine
Davon Isaias sagt
Hat uns gebracht alleine
Marie, die reine Magd.
Aus Gottes ew'gem Rat,
Hat sie ein Kind geboren,
Und blieb doch reine Magd.

Maria Walks amid the Thorn / Maria durch ein Dornwald ging

German carol

Medieval

Ma — ri — a walks a — mid the thorn, Ky—rie e—lei—
Ma — ri — a durch ein' Dorn–wald ging, Ky—rie e—lei—

son. Ma — ri — a walks a — mid the thorn, Which sev — en years no
son. Ma — ri — a durch ein' Dorn — wald ging, Der hat in siebn Jahrn kein

leaf has born. Je — sus and Ma — ri — a. ri — a.
Laub ge-tragn. Je — sus und Ma — ri — a. ri — a.

What 'neath her heart doth Mary bear?
Kyrie eleison.
A little child doth Mary bear,
Beneath her heart He nestles there.
Jesus and Maria.

And as the two are passing near,
Kyrie eleison,
Lo! roses on the thorns appear,
Lo! roses on the thorns appear.
Jesus and Maria.

Was trug Maria unter ihrem Herzen?
Kyrie eleison.
Ein kleines Kindlein ohne Schmerzen,
Das trug Maria unter ihrem Herzen.
Jesus und Maria.

Da habn die Dornen Rosen getragn.
Kyrie eleison.
Als das Kindlein durch den Wald getragn,
Da habn die Dornen Rosen getragn.
Jesus und Maria.

The Christmas Nightingale / Die Weihnachtsnachtigall

German carol

Allegretto

Seventeenth century

Sweet night—in—gale a—wake, A — wake, come forth fair war—bler now, High in the tree on
Fly to the man—ger here, O feath—er'd sis—ter, take thy flight, Sing joy—ous songs with
Lieb Nach—ti—gall, wach auf, Wach auf, du schö—nes Vö—ge—lein, Auf je—nem grü—nen
Flieg her zum Kripp—lein klein, Flieg her ge—fie—dert Schwe—ster—lein, Lass tö—nen hold dein

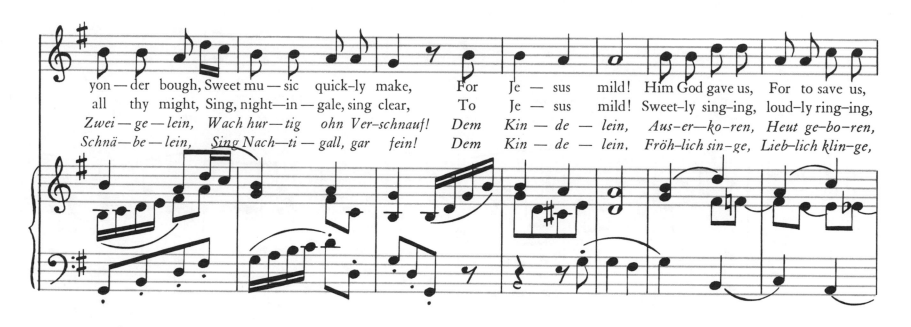

yon — der bough, Sweet mu — sic quick-ly make, For Je — sus mild! Him God gave us, For to save us,
all thy might, Sing, night—in — gale, sing clear, To Je — sus mild! Sweet—ly sing-ing, loud—ly ring-ing,
Zwei — ge — lein, Wach hur — tig ohn Ver-schnauf! Dem Kin — de — lein, Aus-er-ko-ren, Heut ge-bo-ren,
Schnä — be — lein, Sing Nach—ti — gall, gar fein! Dem Kin — de — lein, Fröh-lich sin-ge, Lieb-lich klin-ge,

He for-gave us. Sing, sing, sing, Sing and praise the Ho — ly Child!
Gai-ly wing-ing.
Halb er—fro—ren, Sing, sing, sing, Sing dem zar — ten Je — su-lein!
Flüg-lein schwin-ge.

From Heaven High / Vom Himmel hoch

German carol

Hymn by Martin Luther (1483-1546); harmonization by J. S. Bach (1685-1750)

From heav—en high I come to earth With joy—ful news of Je—sus' birth. So sing ye all and cease to mourn, To us this day a Child is born.

Vom Him—mel hoch da komm ich her, Ich bring euch gu—te neu—e Mär. Der gu—ten Mär bring ich so viel, Da—von ich singn und sa—gen will.

This day the Virgin bore a son,
The best-beloved of ev'ryone,
A precious little baby boy,
To bring to man delight and joy.

All praise to God enthroned on high,
His only Son we glorify.
The angel host brings Christian cheer,
And singing hails a good New Year.

Euch ist ein Kindlein heut geborn
Von einer Jungfrau auserkorn,
Ein Kindelein so zart und fein,
Das soll eur Freud und Wonne sein.

Lob, Ehr sei Gott im höchsten Thron
Der uns schenkt seinen ein' gen Sohn,
Des freuen sich der Engel Schar,
Und singen uns solch neues Jahr.

Christmas Song | Zu Weihnachten

German carol

Poem by Paul Gerhardt (1607-1676); music by J. S. Bach (1685-1750)

Andante molto

I stand be — side Thy cra — dle here, O Je — sus–Child, to ten — der Thee

Ich steh an dei — ner Krip — pe hier, O Je — su–lein, mein Le — ben. Ich

all which Thou hast giv — en me, Which I to Thee sur — ren — der. Take

ste — he, bring und schen — ke dir, Was du mir hast ge — ge — ben. Nimm

then my spir — it, take my soul, My heart and mind in Thy con-trol, And

hin, es ist mein Geist und Sinn, Herz, Seel und Mut, nimm al — les hin, Und

gra—cious—ly re — ceive them.

lass dir's wohl ge — fal — len.

In darkness black, in death I lay,
Thou Sun, dispell'd my sadness.
Thou broughtest heav'nly light of day,
A life of joy and gladness.
O sun, how beautiful Thy rays,
The holy words of faith I praise.
O Lord, I do believe them.

Ich lag in tiefster Todesnacht,
Du wurdest meine Sonne,
Die Sonne die mir zugebracht
Licht, Leben, Freud und Wonne.
O Sonne, die das werte Licht
Des Glaubens in mir zugericht,
Wie schön sind Deine Strahlen!

O Tannenbaum!

German carol

Traditional

O Tan–nen–baum, o
O Tan–nen–baum, o

Tan–nen–baum, your leaves are ev — er faith–ful! Not on — ly green when sum–mer glows, But in the win — ter
Tan–nen–baum, wie treu sind dei—ne Blät–ter! Du grünst nicht nur zur Som–mers–zeit, Nein, auch im Win—ter,

when it snows.　　O　Tan-nen-baum, o　Tan-nen-baum, your leaves are ev — er　faith—ful!
wenn es schneit.　　O　Tan-nen-baum, o　Tan-nen-baum, wie　treu sind dei — ne　Blät—ter!

O Tannenbaum, o Tannenbaum, you are the tree most loved!
How oft you've given me delight
When Christmas fires were burning bright!
O Tannenbaum, o Tannenbaum, you are the tree most loved!

O Tannenbaum, o Tannenbaum, your faithful leaves will teach me
That hope and love and constancy
Give joy and peace eternally.
O Tannenbaum, o Tannenbaum, your faithful leaves will teach me!

O Tannenbaum, o Tannenbaum, du kannst mir sehr gefallen!
Wie oft hat nicht zur Weihnachtszeit
Ein Baum von dir mich hoch erfreut!
O Tannenbaum, o Tannenbaum, du kannst mir sehr gefallen!

O Tannenbaum, o Tannenbaum, dein Kleid soll mich was lehren!
Die Hoffnung und Beständigkeit
Gibt Trost und Kraft zu aller Zeit.
O Tannenbaum, o Tannenbaum, dein Kleid soll mich was lehren!

As Each Happy Christmas / Alle Jahre wieder

German carol

Nineteenth century

As each hap—py Christ — mas Dawns on earth a — gain, Comes the ho — ly
Al — le Jah—re wie — der Kommt das Chris — tus — kind, Auf die Er — de

Christ — child To the hearts of men.

nie — der, Wo die Men—schen sind.

Enters with his blessing
Into ev'ry home
Guides and guards our footsteps
As we go and come.

All unknown, beside me
He will ever stand,
And will safely lead me
With His own right hand.

Kehrt mit seinem Segen
Ein in jedes Haus,
Geht auf allen Wegen
Mit uns ein und aus.

Geht auch mir zur Seite,
Still und unerkannt,
Dass es treu mich leite
An der lieben Hand.

O Come, Little Children / Ihr Kinderlein, kommet

German carol

Poem by Christoph von Schmid (1768-1854); melody by Johann Abraham Peter Schulz (1747-1800)

O come, lit—tle chil—dren, o come, one and all! O come to the cra—dle in Beth—le—hem's stall! And

Ihr Kin—der—lein, kom—met, o kom—met doch all! Zur Krip—pe her—kom—met in Beth—le—hem's Stall, Und

see what the Fa — ther, from high heav'n a—bove, Has sent us to—

seht, was in die — ser hoch—hei — li—gen Nacht Der Va — ter im

1. 2.

3.

night as a proof of His love. there.

Him — mel für Freu — de uns macht. *Chor.*

1. 2.

3.

73

O see in the cradle this night in the stall,
See here wondrous light that is dazzling to all.
In clean lovely white lies the heavenly Child.
Not even the angels are more sweet and mild.

O see where He's lying, the heavenly Boy!
Here Joseph and Mary behold Him with joy;
The shepherds have come, and are kneeling in pray'r,
While songs of the angels float over Him there.

O seht in der Krippe im nächtlichen Stall,
Seht hier bei des Lichtleins hellglänzendem Strahl,
In reinlichen Windeln das himmlische Kind,
Viel schöner und holder als Engel es sind.

Da liegt es, o Kinder, auf Heu und auf Stroh,
Maria und Josef betrachten es froh;
Die redlichen Hirten knien betend davor,
Hoch oben schwebt jubelnd der Engelein Chor.

Maria on the Mountain / Maria auf dem Berge

German carol

Andante dolce

Traditional

On the moun—tain the wind blow—eth wild,   Ma—
Auf dem Ber — ge da ge—het der Wind,   *Da*

ri — a is rock—ing her Child. She rocks Him with her snow — white hand, No
wiegt die Ma—ri — a ihr Kind. Sie wiegt es mit ih—rer schnee—weis — sen Hand, Sie

(*ad libitum* Solo, Soprano or Alto)

oth-er the cra — dle can at-tend. 'O Jo—seph, dear — est Jo—seph mine, O help me to rock my
braucht da—zu kein Wie—gen-band. 'Ach Jo — ſef, lie — ber Jo — ſef mein, Ach hilf mir wie-gen mein

Who's Knocking There? / Wer klopfet an?

Austrian carol

Traditional

Energico

'Who's knock—ing there?'   'Two folk   in   sor—ry
'Wer   klop—fet   an?'   *'O,   zwei   gar   ar—me*

plight.'   'What   seek   ye   here?'   'A   shel—ter   for   the   night.
Leut!'   *'Was wollt   ihr   dann?'*   *'O,   gebt   uns   Her—berg   heut!*

For   God's love   do   not for — sake us,   To   your lodg—ing — house now   take   us.' 'O
O,   *durch Got — tes   Lieb wir bit-ten,   Öff — net uns doch   eu — re   Hüt—ten.'* 'O

no,   o   no!'   'O   force us   not   to   go!'   'It   must   be   so.'   'Our   thank-ful–
nein,   o   nein!'   'O   las—set   uns   doch   ein!'   'Das   kann nicht   sein.'   'Wir   wol—len

ness we'll show.'   'No, it can—not be, I fear; So   now   be   off, you'll   not   stay
dank—bar sein.'   'Nein, das kann ein — mal nicht sein; Drum   packt euch   fort,   ihr   kommt nicht

marcato

1.   **Fine**

here!'
'rein.'

1.   **Fine**

'You come too late.' 'So all the people say.'
'Why do you wait?' 'Ah, only once, today.
For tomorrow comes the Saviour,
To reward your kind behavior.'
' 'Tis naught to me.' 'Our wretched plight now see.'
'What's that to me?' 'Dear Sir, have sympathy!'
'Hold your peace, plague me no more,
Now go! I want to close my door.'

'Ihr kommt zu spät!' 'So heisst es überall.'
'Da geht nur, geht!' 'O Herr, nur heut einmal!
Morgen wird der Heiland kommen,
Dieser liebt und lohnt die Frommen.'
'Geht mich nichts an!' 'Seht unser Elend an!'
'Liegt mir nichts dran.' 'Habt Mitleid, lieber Mann.'
'Schwätzt nicht viel, lasst mich in Ruh,
Da geht! Ich schliess die Türe zu.'

Shepherds, Up! / Hirten, auf um Mitternacht!

Austrian carol

Traditional

Shep — herds, up, your watch to take! Your time of sleep is end — ing,
Hir — ten, auf um Mit — ter-nacht, Er — hebt euch aus dem Schla — fe!

For the Good Shep — herd is a — wake, His earth — ly flock at — tend — ing.
Auf! Der gu — te Hir — te wacht Zu wei — den sei — ne Scha — fe.

Haste to the man—ger, to Ma—ry, so mild, Come and a—dore Him, the heav—en—ly Child!
Eilt zu Ma — ri — a, zum Kripp-lein ge—schwind, Kom—met und grüs—set das gött — li—che Kind!

The Darkness Is Falling / Es wird scho glei dumpa

Austrian carol

Traditional

sweet lul—la—by. Thou art not yet sleep-ing, I hear Thy soft cry. Bye,
slum—ber the best, As tran-quil and qui—et I take me to rest. Hei,
Liab—ling dem Kloan. Du magst jå net schlåfn, i hör di nur woan. Hei,
sor—gen-los sein. Åft kann i mi ruah—li aufs Nie—der—legn freun.

bye, bye, bye, sleep sweet, dear—est Child.
hei, hei, hei, schlaf süass, herz—liabs Kind!

Carol of the Children of Bethlehem / Lied der Kinder zu Bethlehem

Austrian carol

Traditional

We bid Thee
Round Thy poor
Bist ein — mal
Liegst hier im

wel—come, Thou Sav—iour of all,
cra—dle there blows the night air,
kom—men, du Hei—land der Welt,
Stal—le, geht Wind aus und ein,

Born to re—deem us, in dark sta—ble stall.
No lit—tle ba—by would wish to be there.
Uns zu er — lö—sen, wie Mut—ter er—zählt.
Wä — re ich du, o da möcht' ich nicht sein.

Cold is Thy cra — dle, though warm is Thy heart,
Straw is the pil — low on which Thou must rest.
Zit—terst vor Käl—te und liebst uns so warm.
Stroh nur zum Bett—lein, so ärm — lich willst ruhn!

Rich Thou in bless—ings, though
Would we might give Thee of
Bist nicht der Reich—ste, was
Wärst du bei uns ich wollt

pau — per Thou art.
all things the best.
macht dich so arm?
al — les dir tun.

Silent Night / Weihnachtslied

Austrian carol

Music by Franz Gruber (1787-1863)

Lento

Si — lent night! Ho — ly night! All is calm,
Stil — le Nacht! Hei — li—ge Nacht! Al — les schläft,

all is bright, Round yon Vir — gin Moth — er and Child. Ho — ly In — fant, so
ein — sam wacht Nur das trau — te, hei — li—ge Paar. Hol—der Kna—be im

ten — der and mild,
Sleep   in heav — en—ly peace!
Sleep   in heav — en—ly

lok — ki—gen Haar,
Schla — fe in himm — li-scher Ruh!
Schla — fe in himm — li—scher

peace!
Sleep   in heav — en—ly peace!

Ruh!
Schla — fe in himm — li—scher Ruh!

Sleep   in   heav — en—ly   peace!
Schla — fe   in himm — li—scher Ruh!

Silent Night! Holy Night!
Son of God, love's pure light,
Radiant beams from Thy holy face,
With the dawn of redeeming grace,
Jesus, Lord, at Thy birth!

Stille Nacht, heilige Nacht!
Gottes Sohn, o wie lacht
Lieb aus deinem göttlichen Mund,
Da uns schlägt die rettende Stund',
Jesus, in deiner Geburt.

Angels We Have Heard on High / Les Anges dans nos Campagnes

French carol

Traditional

An — gels we have heard on high, sweet — ly sing — ing o'er the plains,
Les an — ges dans nos cam-pa-gnes ont en-ton-né l'hym — ne des cieux,

And the moun — tains in re—ply e — cho — ing their joy — ous strains:
Et l'é — cho de nos mon-ta-gnes re — dit ce chant mé — lo — di—eux:

ri—a   in   ex — cel — sis   De ——————————————— *o.*

Shepherds, why this jubilee?
Why your joyous strains prolong?
What the gladsome tidings be
Which inspire your heav'nly song?   *Refrain*

Come to Bethlehem and see
Him whose birth the angels sing;
Come, adore on bended knee
Christ, the Lord, the new-born King.   *Refrain*

Bergers, pour qui cette fête?
Quel est l'objet de tous ces chants?
Quel vainqueur, quelle conquête
Mérite ces cris triomphants?   Refrain

Ils annoncent la naissance
Du libérateur d'Israel,
Et, pleins de reconnaissance,
Chantent en ce jour solennel!   Refrain

Born Is Jesus, the Infant King / Il est né, le Divin Enfant

French carol

Traditional

Born is Je—sus, the In—fant King,   Play mer—ry o — boes, sweet pipes re—sound—ing;
Il   est né,   le Di — vin En—fant,   Jou — ez haut-bois, ré—son — nez mu—set — tes;

Born is Je — sus, the In—fant King,   Come His   Ad—vent on   earth to sing!   More than four thou-sand
Il   est né,   le Di—vin En—fant,   Chan—tons tous son a — vè—ne—ment.   De—puis plus de qua—

years' de—lay, Since the proph — ets of God fore — told Him. More than four thou—sand years' de—lay
tre mille ans   Nous le pro — met-taient les   pro — phè—tes. De—puis plus de   qua—tre mille ans

rit.

D.C. al Fine

Pass'd   be—fore this all—joy—ful   day.
Nous   at — ten—dions cet   heu—reux temps.

D.C. al Fine

rit.

Born is Jesus, . . .
Ah, how fair is the Child we sing,
How delightful to behold Him.
Ah, how fair is the Child we sing,
He is lovely, the Infant King!

Il est né, . . .
Qu'il est beau, qu'il est charmant,
Que ses grâces sont parfaites.
Qu'il est beau, qu'il est charmant,
Qu'il est doux, ce Divin Enfant.

Bring Your Torches, Jeannette, Isabella / Un Flambeau, Jeannette, Isabelle

French carol

Traditional

Allegretto

Bring your torch-es, Jean—nette, Is-a — bel — la, Bring your torch-es, come hur-ry and run!

Un flam—beau, Jean—nette, I—sa — bel — le, Un flam—beau, cou—rons au ber—ceau!

It is Je—sus, good folk of the vil — lage, Christ is born, and Ma — ry's call — ing, Ah!

C'est Jé—sus, bon—nes gens du ha-meau, Le Christ est né, Ma—rie ap — pel — le, Ah!

ah!   beau—ti—ful   is   the   Moth — er!   Ah!   ah!   beau—ti—ful   is   her   Son!

ah!   que   la   mère   est   bel — le,   Ah!   ah!   ah! que l'En—fant   est   beau!

Skies are glowing, the night is cloudless,
Skies are glowing, come rise from your beds!
Hasten all who would see the dear Christ Child
Shining and bright as yon lone star!
Run! run! put on your finest garments!
Run! run! presents for Jesus bring!

It is wrong, when the Baby is sleeping,
It is wrong to cry out so loud;
Silence, all, as you come near the stable,
Lest your noise should waken Jesus!
Hush! hush! peacefully now he slumbers;
Hush! hush! peacefully now he sleeps.

C'est un tort quand l'Enfant sommeille,
C'est un tort de crier si fort.
Taisez-vous, l'un et l'autre, d'abord!
Au moindre bruit, Jésus s'éveille.
Chut! chut! chut! il dort à merveille.
Chut! chut! chut! voyez comme il dort!

Doucement, dans l'étable close,
Doucement, venez un moment!
Approchez! que Jésus est charmant!
Comme il est blanc, comme il est rose!
Do! do! do! que l'Enfant repose!
Do! do! do! qu'il rit en dormant!

Whence, O Shepherd Maiden? / D'où viens-tu, Bergère?

French carol

Seventeenth century

Whence, o shep-herd maid-en, whence come you? Whence, o shep-herd maid-en, whence come you?

D'où viens — tu, ber—gè—re, d'où viens—tu? D'où viens — tu, ber—gè—re, d'où viens—tu?

I come from the man—ger, walk-ing on my way, Noth-ing ev—er stran—ger seen with—in my day.

Je viens de l'é—ta — ble de m'y pro-me-ner, J'ai vu un mi—ra — cle ce soir ar-ri — ver.

What saw you there, maiden, what saw you?
I saw lying cradled there a tiny Child,
In the new straw huddled softly It was piled.

Was He fair then, maiden, was He fair?
Fairer than the moon is, fairer than the sun,
Never in the world was fairer Child shone on.

Nothing more then, maiden, nothing more?
Mary, holy mother, nursing Babe at breast,
Joseph, holy father, with the cold oppressed.

Qu'as-tu vu, bergère, qu'as-tu vu?
J'ai vu dans la crèche un petit enfant,
Sur la paille fraîche mis bien tendrement.

Est-il beau, bergère, est-il beau?
Plus beau que la lune, aussi le soleil;
Jamais dans le monde on vit son pareil.

Rien de plus, bergère, rien de plus?
Sainte Marie, sa mère, qui lui fait boire du lait,
Saint Joseph, son père, qui tremble de froid.

From Starry Skies Descending / Tu scendi dalle Stelle

Italian carol

Poem by Pope Pius IX (1846-1878); traditional melody

From star—ry skies de-scend — ing, Thou com—est, glo—rious King, A man-ger low Thy
Tu scen—di dal—le stel — le, o Re del Cie — lo, E vieni in u—na

bed, in win—ter's i — cy sting; O my dear—est Child most ho — ly,
grot — ta al fred — do, al ge — lo; O Bam—bi — no mi-o di —vi — no,

Shudd-'ring, trem-bling in the cold! Great God, Thou lov—est me! What suff—'ring Thou didst

Io ti ve—do qui tre—mar ... O Di–o be—a — to, Oh! quan—to ti co-

bear, that I near Thee might be!

sto l'a — ver—mi ama — to!

Thou art the world's Creator, God's own and true Word,
Yet here no robe, no fire for Thee, Divine Lord.
Dearest, fairest, sweetest Infant,
Dire this state of poverty.
The more I care for Thee,
Since Thou, o Love Divine, will'st now so poor to be.

A te, che sei del mondo il Creatore,
Mancano panni e fuoco, o mio Signore
Caro, eletto Pargoletto,
Quanto questa povertà
Piu mi innamora,
Giacche si fece amor povero ancora!

Carol of the Bagpipers / Canzone d'i Zampognari

Italian carol

Traditional

When Christ our Lord was born at Beth—le—hem a—
Quan—no na—scet—te Nin—no a Bet—te—lem—

far, Al—though 'twas night, there shone as bright as noon a star. Nev-er so
me, E—ra not—te e pa—re-a mmie—zo juor—no. Ma—je le

bright—ly, nev—er so white—ly, Shone the stars, as on that night! The bright—est star
stel—le, lu—ste—re e bel—le, Se ve — det—te—ro ac—cus—sì! La chiù lu—cen—

went A—way to call the Wise Men from the O—ri—ent.
te Jet—te a chiam—mà li Ma — gi, in O—ri—en — te.

Herod Dead / Morto Erode

Italian carol

Seventeenth century

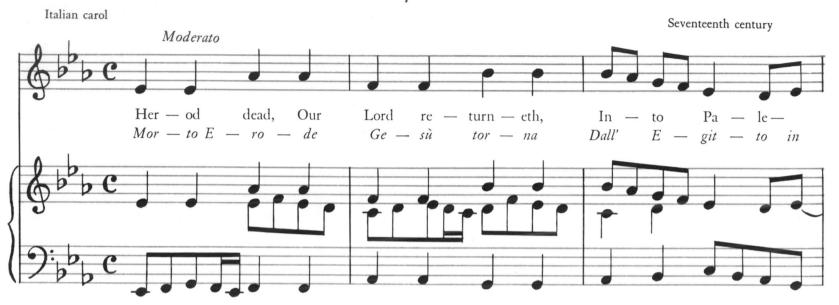

Her — od dead, Our Lord re — turn — eth, In — to Pa — le —
Mor — to E — ro — de Ge — sù tor — na Dall' E — git — to in

stine di — rec — ted, And in Na — za — reth He dwell — eth,
Pa — le — sti — na, Ed a Na — za — reth sog — gior — na,

At a moun—tain's foot e—rec—ted. was greet—ed.
Bor — *go a pié d'u* — *na col—li—na.* *Na* — *za* — *re* — *no.*

All the village was well treated,
Every house with flowers abounding,
Jesus lived in this surrounding,
As a Nazarene was greeted.

Era il borgo molto ameno,
Lieto d'orti fra le case,
E Gesù ch'ivi rimase
Fu poi detto Nazareno.

Fum, Fum, Fum

born of Vir—gin Ma—ry In this night so cold and drea-ry. Fum, fum, fum. He is Na-ci— fum.

la Vir-gen Ma — ri—a en es — ta no-che tan fri—a.

Birds of ev'ry forest grove, sing fum, fum, fum,
All your fledglings on the bough,
Oh, leave them now, oh, leave them now;
For to make a downy cover
For our Jesus, round Him hover.
Fum, fum, fum.

Shining stars from heav'n above, sing fum, fum, fum,
Looking down where Jesus cries,
Oh, come rejoice, oh, come rejoice;
Come and light the night's obscureness
With your light and dazzling pureness.
Fum, fum, fum.

Pajaritos de los bosques, fum, fum, fum,
vuestros hijos de coral
abandonad, abandonad
y formad un muelle nido
a Jesús recién nacido.
Fum, fum, fum.

Estrellitas de los cielos, fum, fum, fum,
que a Jesús miráis llorar
y no lloráis, y no lloráis,
alumbrad la noche oscura
con vuestra luz clara y pura.
Fum, fum, fum.

The Rocking of the Child | El Rorro

Mexican carol

dolcissimo

Traditional

A la ru—ru—ru, my Ba—by dear—est, O sleep, my Je — sus, sleep, my fair — est.
A la ru—ru—ru, ni—ño chi—qui—to, duer—ma—se ya mi Je — su — si — to.

From e—le—phant to fly, no noise be—fore Him, Your si—lence keep, we all shall now a — dore Him. A la ru—
Del e—le—fan—te has—ta el mos—qui—to, Guar—den si — len—cio, no le ha—gan rui— do. A la ru—

ru — ru, my Ba — by dear — est, O sleep, my Je — sus, sleep my fair — est.
ru — ru, ni — ño chi — qui — to, Duer—ma—se ya mi Je — su — si — to.

A la ru-ru-ru, my Baby dearest,
O sleep, my Jesus, sleep my fairest.
O night of gladness, night of exaltation;
Blessed by sweet Mary, Queen of God's creation.   *Refrain*

A la ru-ru-ru, my Baby dearest,
O sleep, my Jesus, sleep my fairest.
The heav'nly choir in accents sweetly ringing,
The tidings of this wondrous birth are singing.   *Refrain*

A la ru-ru-ru, niño chiquito,
Duermase ya mi Jesusito.
Noche venturosa, noche de alegría,
Bendita la dulce, divina María.   Refrain

A la ru-ru-ru, niño chiquito,
Duermase ya mi Jesusito.
Coros celestiales, con su dulce acento,
Canten la ventura de este nacimiento.   Refrain

A la Nanita Nana

Spanish carol

Traditional

Andante ritmico

A   la na—ni—ta   na—na,   na—ni—ta   e — a,   na—ni—ta e — a,

My   Je—sus, He   is   sleep—ing,   o come be — hold   Him, o   come be—hold   Him.

Mi   Je—sús tie — ne   sue — ño,   ben—di—to   se — a,   ben—di—to   se — a.

Lit—tle brook ev—er—flow—ing, rush—ing and ring—ing,
Fuen—te—ci—lla que co—rres cla — ra y so — no — ra,

Night—in—gale in the for—est,
rui—se—ñor q'en la sel — va

sigh — ing and sing—ing,
can — tan—do llo—ras,

Qui — et now, while the cra—dle
ca—llad mien—tras la cu—na

soft — ly en — folds Him.
se ba—lan — ce — a.

A la na—ni—ta na—na, na—ni—ta e — a.

Refrain
O thou tragic foreboding of the sad morrow,
Shadow of coming anguish, suff'ring and sorrow,
Fly, shadows, while the cradle softly enfolds Him.
Refrain

Refrain
Y tú triste presagio que me torturas,
almácigo de penas y de amarguras,
huye mientras la cuna se balancea. Refrain

Refrain
Fair as violets and roses, Baby beguiling,
Say what visions surround Thee, why art Thou smiling?
Ah, what appears before Thee, Infant so lowly?
Softly Thy sweet lips murmur: "Sacrament Holy." *Refrain*

Refrain
I know not to explain it, sorrow has vanished,
O Thy smile, little Jesus, my care has banished.
Dream, dream, o gentle Master, dreams without number,
Let no affliction trouble Thy peaceful slumber. *Refrain*

Refrain
Singing birds, flowing fountains, winds gently blowing,
Silence, for He is sleeping, cheeks brightly glowing,
Quiet now, while the cradle softly enfolds Him,
My Holy Child is sleeping, come and behold Him. *Refrain*

Refrain
Manojito de rosas y de alelíes,
qué es lo que estás soñando, que te sonríes?
Cuáles son tus ensueños, dilo alma mia;
mas qué es lo que murmuras? "Eucaristía." Refrain

Refrain
Yo no sé lo que es eso, Niño del alma,
mas pues esa sonrisa mis penas calma,
sigue, sigue soñando mi dulce Dueño,
sin que nada te ahuyente tan dulce sueño. Refrain

Refrain
Pajaritos y fuentes, auras y brisas,
respetad ese sueño y esas sonrisas,
callad mientras la cuna se balancea;
que el Niño está soñando, bendito sea! Refrain

Mary the Virgin to Bethlehem Went / Jungfru Maria till Betlehem gick

Swedish carol

Andante

Early eighteenth century

Ma–ry the Vir—gin to Beth—le—hem went.
Ma–ry the Vir—gin a dream did be — hold.
Jung—fru Ma–ri — a   till Bet —le—hem gick.
Jung—fru Ma–ri — a fick en sömn så   söt.

Prais'd   be God's ho—ly name ev—er—more!
Lo — vat va—re Guds he—li—ga namn!

Je — sus she   bore   by   her   con–sent.
She bore the   Son   that   was   fore–told.
Je — sus, kär   son — en,   där   hon fick.
Je — sus, kär   son-en fran   hen — ne gick.

The Ho — ly Ghost we   a — dore.
Och så   den he—li — ge and'!

Dance Carol / Nu är det Jul igen

Swedish dance carol

Traditional

Allegro

Yule–tide is here a–gain, and Yule–tide is here a–gain, and Hap — py days we'll have till Eas — ter.
Nu är det Jul i—gen, och Nu är det Jul i—gen, och Ju — len va—ra ska' till Pås — ka.

Bass staccato throughout

Then there is Eas—ter—tide, and Then there is Eas—ter—tide, and Hap — py days we'll have till Christ—mas.
Så är det Påsk i—gen, och Så är det Påsk i—gen, och Påsk—en va—ra ska' till Ju — la.

Yule—tide is here a—gain, and Yule—tide is here a—gain, and Hap—py days we'll have till Eas—ter.
Nu är det Jul i—gen, och Nu är det Jul i—gen, och Ju—len va—ra ska' till Pås—ka.

This is not the truth, and This is not the truth, for Lent comes in be—tween and fast—ing.
Det var in — te sant, och Det var in—te sant, för Där e—mel—lan kom—mer Fas—tan.

Saint Stephen Was Riding / Staffansvisa

Swedish carol

Traditional

Saint Ste — phen was rid—ing and he trav — el'd a—
Sankt Staf — fan han ri—der si — na häs — tar till

far, Watch with us this Christ—mas night! When from the rich O — rient he
vanns, Va — ka med oss Ju — la—natt! Då såg han en stjär — na i

saw a glow—ing star. Watch with us and pray with us all!

Ös — terns ri — ka land. Va — ka med oss för oss al — la!

The star brightly o'er the town of Bethlehem shone, *Refrain*
Ablaze o'er the house where He lay, the Holy One. *Refrain*

Saint Stephen to Herod went, the king in his might, *Refrain*
'One greater than thou has been born this holy night!' *Refrain*

'Thy words I'll not credit and their truth I'll not know,' *Refrain*
'Until yonder rooster flies up and starts to crow!' *Refrain*

The rooster was roasted and in gravy he lay, *Refrain*
He rose up and crowed as he crowed at break of day! *Refrain*

Den stjärnan lyste över Betlehems stad. Refrain
Men mäst över huset, där barnet det var. Refrain

Sankt Staffan sig inför Herodes måste gå. Refrain
I natt är en födder, som bättre är än du. Refrain

Säg, hur skall jag tro dig uppå dessa dina ord? Refrain
Förran den hanen han flyger upp och gal. Refrain

Den hanen var stekter och laggder uppå fat. Refrain
Han baskade sina vingar så högt som han gal. Refrain

Come All Ye Shepherds / Nesem vám noviny

Czech carol

Traditional

Come, all ye shep — herds, come hark un — to me!
Ne — sem vám no — vi — ny, po — slou — chej — te,

Go ye to Beth — le — hem, Je — sus to see! Great is the sto—ry,
z bet—lem — ské Kra — ji — ny, po — zor dej — te. Slyš — te je pil—ně

great is His glo—ry, Great is the sto—ry, great is His glo—ry, Be not a — fraid!

a ne—o—myl—ně, slyš — te je pil—ně a ne—o—myl—ně roz — jí—mej — te.

Let us obey now the heavenly voice!
Jesus, our Saviour's born. Come and rejoice!
Come every nation, give adoration,
Gifts to Him present!

Truly the angels have spoken today:
See Mary, Jesus, the stable, the hay!
Hear their sweet singing, round us now ringing,
Glory on high!

*K němužto andělé s nebe přišli,
i také pastýři jsou se sešli,
Jeho vítali, jeho chválili,
dary nesli.*

*Žádáme srdečnou zkroušeností,
by Jsi nás uvedl do radosti
tam kde přebýváš, slávy požíváš,
na věčnosti.*

Rocking Song / Hajej, nynej, Ježíšku

Czech lullaby carol

Traditional

Lit—tle Je—sus, sweet—ly sleep, do not stir; We will lend a coat of fur.
Ha—jej, ny—nej, Je — žiš—ku, Je — žiš—ku, pu — či—me ti Ko — žiš—ku.

We will rock you, rock you, rock you, We will rock you, rock you, rock you.
Bu—de—me tě Ko — li — ba — ti, 'a—bys moh' li — bě po—spa — ti,

See the fur to keep you warm, Snug — ly round your ti — ny form.
ha — jej, ny — nej, mi — lač — ku, Ma — ri — án — ský sy — náč — ku.

Shepherds, Come A-Running | Przybieżeli do Betleem Pasterze

Polish carol

Traditional

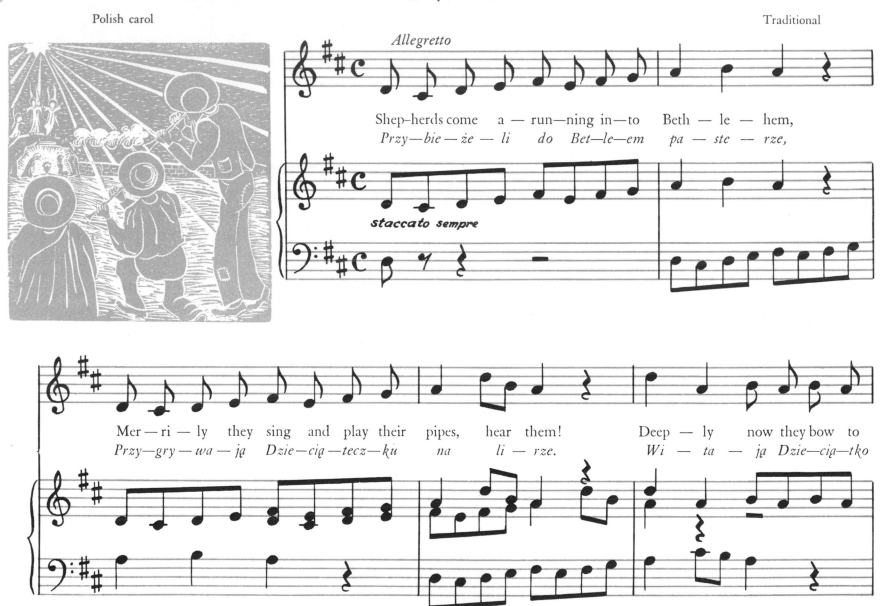

Shep—herds come a—run—ning in—to Beth—le—hem,
Przy—bie—że—li do Bet—le—em pa—ste—rze,

Mer—ri—ly they sing and play their pipes, hear them! Deep—ly now they bow to
Przy—gry—wa—ją Dzie—cią—tecz—ku na li—rze. Wi—ta—ją Dzie—cią—tko

Ma—ry, won-d'ring how to greet the Child,
ma—te, Pa—cho-lą-tko, pas — te — rze,

Je — sus mild.
pas — te — rze.

Deep—ly now they bow to
Wi — ta — ją Dzie-cią—tko

Ma—ry, won-d'ring how to greet the Child,
ma—te. Pa—cho-lą-tko, pa — ste — rze,

1°
Je — sus mild.
pa — ste — rze.

Fine
Je — sus mild.
pa — ste — rze.

Rockabye Jesus / Lulajże Jezuniu

Polish lullaby carol

Traditional

Rock — a — bye Je — sus, my soul's fair—est treas—ure,
Lu — laj — że Je — zu—niu mo — ja per — eł—ko,

Rock — a — bye
Lu — laj u —

Je — sus, my love knows no meas—ure.
lu — bio—ne me pie — ści—deł—ko.

Rock—a — bye Je — sus sweet, close I will
Lu—laj—że Je — zu—niu lu—laj—że

hold Thee, I'll hold Thee, As Ma — ry's lov — ing arms then did en—fold Thee.
lu — laj—że lu—laj, A ty go ma — tu—lu w pła—czu u — tu — laj.

2.

then did en — fold Thee.
w pła—czu u — tu — laj.

Jesus Christ Is Born | Gdy Się Chrystus Rodzi

Polish carol

Traditional

Je—sus Christ is born Now un—to the world. Ev'—ry dark of night Turn—ed in—to
Gdy się Chry—stus ro—dzi I na świat przy — cho—dzi; Ciem—na noc w ja — sno—ściach Pro—mie—ni —stych

light. Hosts of an — gels, hear them sing—ing Hymns of joy, and prais — es ring—ing:
bro—dzi. A — nio — ło — wie się ra—du — ją Pod nie—bio — sy wy — śpie—wu—ją:

Glo — ri—a, glo — ri—a, glo — ri—a in ex—cel—sis De — o!

In the fields the shepherds
By their flocks abiding,
Harkened to the angel:
Hear ye this great tiding!
Go ye, go to Bethle'm yonder,
There to see salvation's wonder:
Gloria . . .

Mowia do pasterzy
Którzy trzód swych strzegli:
Aby do Betlejem
Częmprendzej pobiegli.
Bo się narodził Zbawiciel
Wszego świata Odkupiciel:
Gloria . . .

GLORIA IN EXCELSIS DEO

Notes

p. 9   JERUSALEM REJOICE

The third Sunday of Advent is called "Gaudete Sunday," for the introit of the Mass of that day begins with St. Paul's exhortation: "Rejoice (*Gaudete*) . . . The Lord is nigh" (Phil. 4, 6). At vespers the antiphon *Jerusalem gaude* is sung in the seventh (mixolydian) mode, the mode of exultation and joy. The words are those of the prophet Zacharias (9, 9).

An accompaniment for this and the following plain song is provided for those who cannot do without. Whenever possible, do not use it. Let the chants rise on their own melodic and rhythmic power.

p. 10   JESUS, REDEEMER OF THE WORLD

This hymn has been called a "song of love, of tenderness, of enraptured contemplation." It originated in the Ambrosian School of the 6th century. Its melody in the first (Dorian) mode still resounds today in the liturgical vesper service at Christmas. It is suggested that two half-choirs alternate in singing the stanzas, or a smaller group of singers and the entire chorus. Use no accompaniment unless support by an instrument is absolutely needed.

p. 12   A CHILD IS BORN IN BETHLEHEM

During the Middle Ages many newly created texts, poetry and prose, were added to the ancient Latin liturgy. Frequently new words were inserted in the established phrases, for example: *Kyrie—fons bonitatis—eleison*. Such an insertion (called a trope) was made during the 14th century in the Christmas liturgy, between the priest's words, *Benedicamus Domino* and the response, *Deo gratias* at the close of services. In the Christmas poem, *Puer natus in Bethlehem*, the words still echo the language of the liturgy and the last verse leads into the *Deo gratias*. To the original 14th-century plain song, an upper voice was added which finally, in many different versions, supplanted the older tune. The *Tropus ad Benedicamus*, as this carol was called, was sung in Latin and in the vernacular. Our harmonization is by J. S. Bach (Cantata No. 65).

p. 14   HE, WHOM JOYOUS SHEPHERDS PRAISED

Der Quempass geht um ("the Quempass is going around")—this was the expression used in Germany for several centuries to denote the singing and playing of hymns and carols by choirs and congregations on Christmas morning. The choir members sang from the *Quempass-Heft* ("Quempass Notebook") into which they had carefully copied words and melodies, together with ornaments and drawings referring to the Christmas story.

The first and most important of these songs, called "The Quempass," was bilingual—Latin and German—and its first Latin words explain its title and that of the Notebook: *Quem pastores laudavere*. Words and melody go back to the 14th century and are to be found in many collections from 1555 on.

p. 16   CAROL OF THE NUNS OF SAINT MARY'S, CHESTER

This carol is a unique combination of a Latin Christmas poem and an English lullaby.

The origins of this early carol and of so many other Christmas cradle songs and Christmas lullabies lie in the medieval Christmas custom of "rocking the Child," known all over Europe from the 10th to the 16th century. During Christmas Night girls carried a cradle in procession into the church. An image of the Infant Jesus was put into this cradle and to the ringing of bells and singing of carols by the congregation the girls "rocked the child."

p. 18   O COME, ALL YE FAITHFUL

A carol that belongs not to one nation but to mankind, sung in more than 100 different languages.

The original melody was a plain song used in the monasteries of France. Its present-day version can be traced to a manuscript of John Francis Wade: *Cantus Diversi*, 1746. It was first printed in 1782.

The English translation (one of more than forty) is Frederick Oakeley's (1802-1880).

p. 21   O PUBLISH THE GLAD STORY

The original source of this carol is a popular 17th-century French air, *Amants, quittez vos chaînes*. The melody is used for many carols.

p. 23   SING, O SING

This carol is of German origin, and is preserved in the Swedish collection, *Piae Cantiones*, 1582. There exists no Latin text for the second verse, and a German text is supplied in M. Praetorius' (1571-1621) choral setting on which the present piano part is based.

p. 32   COVENTRY CAROL

This carol was sung in the 15th-century *Pageant of the Shearmen and Tailors* by the women of Bethlehem, just before Herod's soldiers came to slaughter their children. The tune and accompaniment appear here according to the earliest recorded musical version, of 1591.

p. 34   THE HOLLY AND THE IVY

The text of this carol was known in the early 18th century but dates from an earlier period. The tune was collected by Cecil Sharp, rediscoverer of English folksong.

GOOD KING WENCESLAS

This delightful tune was originally a spring song (in *Piae Cantiones*, 1582). J. M. Neale (1818-1866) substituted his Wenceslas poem for the original text. The feast of Saint Stephen is December 26th.

WHAT CHILD IS THIS?

William C. Dix's (1837-1898) poem is set to the "Northern Dittye" (known to Shakespeare) "Greensleeves" by Sir John Stainer (1840-1901).

AS JOSEPH WAS A-WALKING

This is a traditional carol adapted to an American tune of oral tradition by Richard Chase and the folksinger Horton Barker of Chilhowie, Virginia. The Trapp Family Singers received the carol from Richard Chase "in gratitude for an unforgettable concert one cold winter evening in Waynesboro, Virginia."

THE SEVEN JOYS OF MARY

This carol has many different versions, in England as well as in America. Some enumerate up to twelve joys. The text of the "Seven Joys" goes back to 15th-century England and was one of the most popular carols up to the 18th century.

The magnificent air is set down here as sung from oral tradition by Mr. Kit Williamson, near Rustburg, Virginia. The text has been revised by John Powell and Richard Chase.

AWAY IN A MANGER

This is usually called Luther's Cradle Hymn, but neither the words nor the music were written by Luther. The origin of this carol is definitely American, probably in the colony of German Lutherans in Pennsylvania. The poem first appeared in print in Philadelphia in 1885, with the present melody in 1887.

JOY TO THE WORLD

The words of this carol are taken from the *Psalms of David* by the Englishman Isaac Watts (1674-1748). The melody was composed in imitation of the style of G. F. Handel by Lowell Mason of Massachusetts (1792-1872), and first appeared in print in 1839.

MARIA WALKS AMID THE THORN

The *Gesangbuch* of Andernach (1608) refers to this song as one universally known and liked at that time.

The insertion of the words *Kyrie eleison* in this and in the following carol shows that both have their origin in the first period of the creation of German religious folksongs during the Middle Ages.

FROM HEAVEN HIGH

Martin Luther's "a Children's Hymn of the Christ Child for Christmas Eve," 1535. Our harmonization is by J. S. Bach (from the Christmas Oratorio). The third stanza is explained by the fact that in Luther's time Christmas marked the beginning of the New Year.

CHRISTMAS SONG

In 1736, G. C. Schemelli, cantor at the castle of Zeitz, requested J. S. Bach's cooperation on a hymnal of 954 hymns. It was on this occasion that Bach, inspired by the German choral, as well as by the Italian melodic form, composed this lovely sacred aria.

WHO'S KNOCKING THERE?

During Advent and on Christmas Eve, young people go about in the villages of the Austrian Alps, from house to house. They are called the *Anglöckler,* the bellringers, because in pagan times they rang cowbells and played noisy instruments for the purpose of expelling evil spirits and calling forth fertility of soil. Today they announce the birth of Christ, recite the Gospel story, and sing carols. Often they impersonate Mary and Joseph seeking admission into an inn in songs like this one.

SHEPHERDS, UP!

The father of the house starts to sing this carol on Christmas Eve, when it is time to get up for Midnight Mass. The other members of the family gradually join him, at each repeat one step higher. If possible, sing this carol without accompaniment, at least when sung in only two parts. When men's voices are available, they should join in the second half of the carol, taking their notes from the left hand of the piano part. Repeat as often as convenient, always one step higher! In the repeats everybody comes in at the beginning, the tenors singing with the sopranos, the basses with the altos.

THE DARKNESS IS FALLING

One of the prize possessions of nearly every family in the valleys of the Tyrol is the crèche. The figures of Jesus, Mary and Joseph, the shepherds, the Three Wise Men, are carved in wood, often by the people themselves, and are to be seen in the "stable," with the city of Bethlehem in the background, mountains and trees, as magnificent as can be afforded. Around these crèches people gather during all the Christmas season—lasting from the first Sunday in Advent to Candlemas on February 2—and sing carols and lullabies.

SILENT NIGHT

The carol was first performed, to the accompaniment of a guitar, on December 24, 1818, in Arnsdorf, near Salzburg, by the priest, Joseph Mohr, who had written the poem, and the teacher, Franz Gruber, who had composed the music. Our version represents the vocal parts of the autograph copy which the composer made later for a friend, and a reduction, in the piano part, of Gruber's orchestration for strings, French horn and organ. The German title, *Weihnachtslied,* appears on the composer's autograph copy.

FROM STARRY SKIES DESCENDING

This famous poem is set to a much older melody that is closely related to the Neapolitan *Carol of the Bagpipers,* and to the Neapolitan *Canzone di Natale.*

CAROL OF THE BAGPIPERS

During the nine days before Christmas and during the Christmas season, the bagpipers come to Naples from the Abruzzi Mountains and go from house to house playing and singing before the image of the Holy Infant in the creche, or before the madonnas in the street-corner shrines. (Similar customs were once observed in Rome and are still observed in Sicily.) Handel undoubtedly received the inspiration for his aria, "Come unto Him," in his oratorio, *The Messiah,* from this carol.

HEROD DEAD

This is one of the very rare carols that deal with the events reported in the Gospel of St. Matthew (2, 19-23).

FUM, FUM, FUM

"Fum" should be pronounced "foom" with a short vowel, and the "m" should be hummed with energy, to imitate the sound of guitars and the strumming of string instruments.

THE ROCKING OF THE CHILD

Nine evenings before Christmas the Mexican people commemorate the difficult journey of Mary and Joseph from Nazareth to Bethlehem in a celebration called *Posada,* "the Inn." Young and old form a procession to a house, every evening a different one, and ask admission with a song. First they are refused, but upon their telling that it is Mary and Joseph who seek lodging they are admitted. Then follow prayers and more singing and gaiety and dancing. On Christmas Eve, at the last of the Posadas, the Holy Infant is put into the manger and sung to sleep to the sound of *El Rorro.*

A LA NANITA NANA

This is a most unusual carol, combining a tender lullaby with profound thought over a melody and rhythms of popular Latin authenticity. The change from a minor to a major key in the carol is a feature of certain Spanish folksongs, and is also found in some Cuban folksongs (*guajira*). No "bye, bye" nor "lullaby" would do justice to the Spanish phrases of tenderness toward the little Baby. Therefore we decided to abstain from translating them and keep them, in the English verses, just as they are in the original.

MARY THE VIRGIN TO BETHLEHEM WENT

This is an extraordinarily beautiful, early 18th-century melody from Skultuna, Sweden. The invocations repeated in every stanza of this song and also of the *Staffansvisa* reveal the religious celebrations of the Middle Ages as the original source and inspiration of these songs: Christmas Eve is a night spent in meditation, prayer, and singing, leading into the Midnight Mass.

DANCE CAROL

Children and adults dance around their Christmas trees in Sweden, singing this carol. The tune derives from their most popular folkdance, the *Hambo.*

SAINT STEPHEN WAS RIDING

The twenty stanzas of the *Staffansvisa,* one of the oldest folksongs of Sweden, tell the delightful "Miracle of the Cock," based on a story in the apocryphal Gospel of Nicodemus, and end wishing everybody "a glad and happy Yule." The Staffan of the song has the features of two entirely different personalities, those of the deacon, St. Stephen of Jerusalem, whose feast is celebrated on December 26th and therefore closely connected with Christmas, and those of the 11th-century missionary, Staffan, who traveled far in the north. The latter was killed by pagans and an unbroken foal brought his body to Norrala, where a chapel was built over his grave. In all Germanic lands he became the patron of health and of horses, and being confused with St. Stephen of Jerusalem, he shares his honors on December 26th, such as the "Stephen-Cup" drunk to good health, and horseback rides around churches and through villages. On the occasion of such "Stephen's rides" on December 26th, this song is still sung in Skane in Sweden. On Christmas Eve it is sung in Vidtskövle, Sweden. It is one of the most beautiful and interesting melodies among Swedish folksongs.

ROCKABYE JESUS

This is the famous Polish Lullaby Carol. The second part (ad libitum) given here represents the way this carol is sung in Poland.

JESUS CHRIST IS BORN

In many Polish churches this carol is sung first by the men; at the "gloria," the women and children join; the second part is ad libitum.